Stories
of Scotch

Enos A. Mills

Longs Peak, Colo,

Sept, 1, 1922

Temporal Mechanical Press
Longs Peak, Colorado

Introduction

When I was a kid I was enchanted with Scotch, always wanting to hear another Scotch story from any member of my family. He was so smart and did so many clever things with Enos on their adventures. It was fun to be off in the woods and to imagine being with them questing. What it has taken me years to comprehend, is how unusual it is for human beings to treat each other as intelligent, highly functioning brains, much less extend that practice to animals, as Enos did.

One day my Dad brought home a dog who was collie and coyote mix. She was my companion when I played in the forest in all seasons and weather, and inevitably tempted by her nose, she was off on her own adventures, but would check in on me until I was home again. She was my friend and guide, teaching me her perspectives and values.

For most of my life I've been fortunate to have had a dog in my life, they help keep me real. If I feel like an idiot justifying something to them, I know I've jumped off the deep end.

I'm big on the theory that life forms that lack verbal ability don't require it. They communicate in ways our immature mentality can't comprehend. Humans have it because we need it, depend on it, and most of us would be lost without it. When you hang around a bunch of animals you start getting impressions of sensations. Words seems superfluous. They communicate with timely directness to those who take the time and patience to hear.

It starts simply and quietly, when you are quiet inside...untroubled and receptive and creative. The intuitive spirit, guides, where the brain is so curious to explore. It's all about the individual experience, not in doing it a certain way. It's knowing how your senses works together. The sensation of being a meadow away from a coyote, sending a feeling of good day and having the awareness returned to you. Experiencing a universal connection with a moose has nothing to do with how close in proximity you are to it.

The best complement we've received is when our friends tell us they want to come back as one of our dogs. We operate from the logical assumption that if we have a highly functioning brain, every living being must also, behaving with connection and respect as best we can, glad we get to share a bit of life's path together. We feel fortunate that we get to spend a bit of time with these distinctive souls.

Enos gave us so many splendid stories of intelligent behavior from other life forms, to express the potential of the brain. To learn from, to be better than we were yesterday, to share compassion with spirits who look and act different than ourselves, to help create harmony and grace, to treat all brains with honor and dignity, the way we all want to be treated. May the creatures you encounter be joyous at the experience.

Elizabeth
Long's Peak

Estes Park Nov. 18

My Dear Mr. Rodgers:

Am sending you four signed copies of "Story of Scotch." This is 50¢ each — $2.00

very truly yours

Enos A Mills

Preface

Scotch and I were companions through eight years. Winter and summer we explored the rugged mountains of the Continental Divide. Often we were cold; more often we were hungry. Together we fought our way through blizzards and forest fires. Never did he complain and at all times he showed remarkable intelligence and absolute fidelity. The thousands who have watched him play football by my cabin on the slope of Long's Peak and the other thousands who have read of his unusual experiences will be interested, I am sure, in this complete story of his life.

I gave an account of Scotch in my Wild Life on the Rockies, and in The Spell of the Rockies I related one of our winter experiences. These chapters and an article on him which I wrote for Country Life in America are, together with additional matter, embodied in this little book.

Enos A. Mills

To Mary King Sherman and John King Sherman
who knew and appreciated Scotch.

Next Page: Photos from the
Country Life in America article, 1912.

Scotch with his master's skees and snowshoes. He could assume the dignity of a bishop when the occasion demanded

Scotch was a favorite with the small animal life around the house. Chipmunks sometimes romped over him

Stories of Scotch

1

A famous collie and her five little puppies came into the possession of a Swedish farmer of my acquaintance. For an unimportant and forgotten kindness which I had shown his children, he decided that I should have one of these promising puppies. To his delight I chose the "wisest one," wee "Scotch," who afterwards gave pleasure to hundreds of people and who for eight years was a factor in my life.

I carried little Scotch all day long in my overcoat pocket as I rode through the mountains on the way to my cabin. His cheerful, cunning face, his good behavior, and the bright way in which he poked his head out of my pocket, licked my hand, and looked at the scenery, completely won my heart before I had ridden an hour. That night he showed so strikingly the strong, faithful characteristics for which collies are noted that I resolved never to part with him. Since then we have had great years together. We have been hungry and happy together, and together we have played by the cabin, faced danger in the wilds, slept peacefully among the flowers, followed trails by starlight, and cuddled down in winter's drifting snow.

We camped for the night by a dim road near a deserted ranch house in the mountains. Scotch was quiet during the long ride, but while I was lighting the campfire he climbed out of my overcoat and proceeded, puppy fashion, to explore the camp. After one bark at my pony he went over to make her acquaintance. He playfully smelled each of her feet, gave a happy bark, and jumped up to touch her nose with his own. Cricket, the pony, intently watched his performance with lowered head and finally nosed him in a friendly manner.

I shut him up in a small abandoned cabin for the night. He at once objected and set up a terrible barking and howling, gnawing fiercely at the crack beneath the door and trying to tear his way out. Fearing he would break his little puppy teeth, or possibly die from frantic and persistent efforts to be free, I concluded to release him from the cabin. My fears that he would run away if left free were groundless. He made his way to my saddle, which lay on the ground nearby, crawled under it, turned round beneath it, thrust his little head from beneath the arch of the horn, and lay down with a look of contentment, and also with an air which said: "I'll take care of this saddle. I'd like to see any one touch it."

And watch it he did. At midnight a cowboy came to my campfire. He had been thrown from his bronco and was making back to his outfit on foot. Tiny Scotch flew at him ferociously; never have I seen such faithful ferocity in a dog so small and young. I took him in my hands and assured him that the visitor was welcome, and in a moment little Scotch and the cowboy were side by side gazing at the fire.

On our arrival at my cabin he at once took possession of an old tub in a corner of the porch. This he liked, and it remained his kennel for a long time. Here, protected from wind and rain, he was comfortable even in cold weather.

We were intimate from the start, and we lived most of the time apart from the world. I watched his development with satisfaction. He grew rapidly in size, strength, comprehension, and accomplishments. He was watchful and fearless through life.

His first experience with the unfriendly side of life came from a burro. A prospector came by with one of those long-eared beasts. Confiding Scotch went out to play with the burro and was kicked. Thenceforward he looked upon all burros with distrust, and every one that came near the cabin promptly and precipitously retreated before him like a boy before an aggressive bumblebee.

The summer that Scotch was growing up, I raised Johnny, a jolly young grizzly bear. At first the smaller, Johnny early became the larger. Both these youngsters were keenly alert, playful, and inclined to be friendly. Each, however, was a trifle suspicious of the other. Unfortunately, I was away during the period in which a complete understanding between them could have been established and, as a result, there never came about the intimate companionship that really should have existed between these two highly developed animals; but their relations, though ever peculiar, were never strained. At times both had the freedom of the yard at once, and naturally they sometimes met while going to and fro. On these occasions each passed the other by as though unconscious of his presence.

Sometimes they lay at close range for an hour at a time, quietly, half admiringly watching each other. A bone was used as a medium the few times they played together. Each in turn guarded this bone while the other tried to take it away. Scotch was enjoying this, when he discovered Johnny watching him eagerly. Plainly Johnny wanted that bone. After a little while Scotch leaped to his feet, looked off in the direction beyond Johnny and barked, as though some object of interest was coming from that direction. Then, picking up the bone, he walked away. As he passed in front of Johnny he dropped the bone and gave a bark. Going on a short distance, he barked once or twice more and lay down watching this pretended object in the distance. Johnny was more interested in the bone, but Scotch had dropped this a foot or two beyond his reach, chained as he was. For some time Johnny stood with his nose pointing at the bone, apparently thinking deeply as to how he might reach it. At last, stretching his chain to the utmost he reached out with his right arm. But he could not touch it. Although

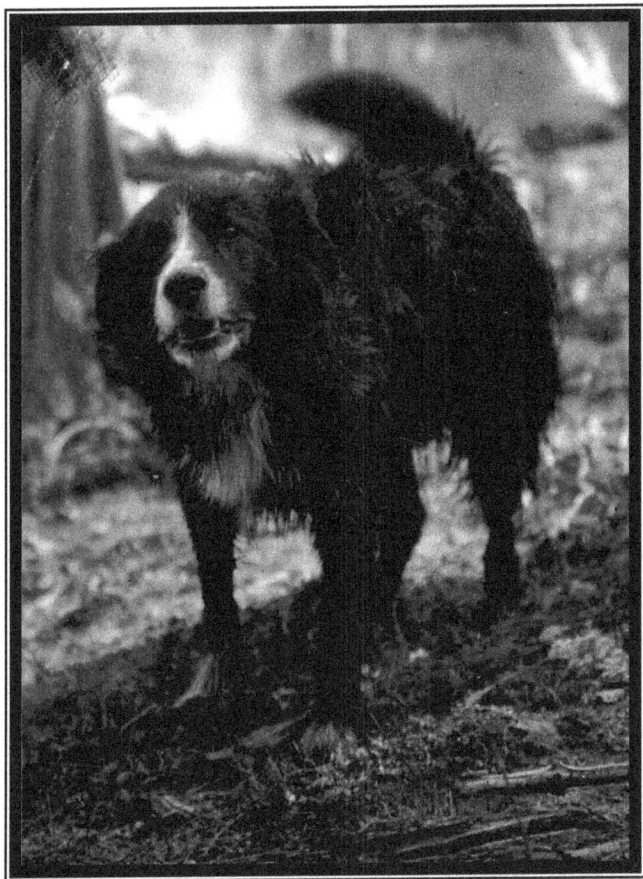

Scotch
Growls

realizing that he probably could not reach it with the left arm, nevertheless he tried.

At this time Scotch was watching Johnny out of the corner of his eye and plainly enjoyed his failures. Johnny stood looking at the bone; Scotch continued looking at Johnny. Suddenly Johnny had an idea. He wheeled about, reached back with his hind foot and knocked the bone forward where he could pick it up with fore paws. Scotch, astonished, leaped to his feet and walked off without a bark or once looking back. This brought out from both a lively lot of striking, feinting, boxing, dodging, and grabbing, which usually ended in clinching and wrestling. Ofttimes they wrestled, and sometimes in their rough and tumble they played pretty roughly. As a climax often Scotch would aim for a neck hold on Johnny and hammer him on the tip of his sensitive nose with one fore paw, while Johnny if possible would seize Scotch's tail in his mouth and shut down on it with his needle-like teeth.

Scotch was an old-fashioned collie and had a face that was exceptionally expressive and pleasing. He was short-nosed, and his fine eyes were set wide apart. When grown he was a trifle larger than the average dog, and was surprisingly agile and powerful for his size. His coat was a shaggy, silky black, with feet, tip of tail, and breast of pure white. He was always well dressed and took good care of his coat and feet. Daily he immersed himself in the cold waters of the brook, when it was not frozen, and he frequently lay in the water, lapping it and enjoying himself.

I never knew of his killing anything, though often in the woods he merrily chased the lively, playful chipmunks. Never, however, did he disturb bird or chipmunk in the yard around the cabin. Often two or three chipmunks romped over him as he lay, with half-shut eyes, near the door. Occasionally, a bird hopped upon him, and frequently birds, chipmunks, and Scotch ate together

Scotch near Long's Peak Inn.

from the same bowl.

Scotch did but little barking. In the country most dogs bow-wow at strangers, and frequently make the night hideous with prolonged barking at far off sounds or imaginary objects. In summer Scotch allowed the scores of daily callers to come and go without a bark, but he reserved the right to announce, with a bark or two, the approach of the semi-occasional stranger who invaded our winter isolation.

I suppose his bravery and watchful spirit may be instinct inherited from his famous forbears who lived so long and so cheerfully on Scotland's heaths and moors. But, with all due respect for inherited qualities, he also has a brain that does a little thinking and meets emergencies promptly and ably.

Talking to animals appears to make them gentler and more responsive. Scotch never tired of listening to me, and I often talked to him as if he were a child. He came to understand many of the words used. If I said "hatchet," he hastened to bring it; if "fire," he at once endeavored to discover where it was. Cheerfully and intelligently he endeavored to help me, and early became efficient in driving cattle, horses, and burros. Instinctively he was a "heeler," and with swift heel nips quickly awakened and gave directions to lazy or unwilling "critters."

ll

Many of Scotch's actions were beyond the scope of instinct. One day, while still young, he mastered a new situation by the use of his wits. While he was alone at the house, some frightened cattle smashed a fence about a quarter of a mile away and broke into the pasture. He was after them in an instant. From a mountainside ledge above, I watched proceedings with a glass. The cattle were evidently excited by the smell of some animal and did not drive well. Scotch ignored the two pasture gates, which were closed, and endeavored to hurry the cattle out through the break through which they had entered. After energetic encouragement, all but one went flying out through the break. This one alternated between stupidly running back and forth along the fence and trying to gore Scotch. Twice the animal had run into a corner by one of the gates, and his starting for the corner the third time apparently gave Scotch an idea. He stopped heeling, raced for the gate, and leaping up, bit at the handle of the sliding wooden bar that secured it. He repeated this biting and tearing at the handle until the bar slid and the gate swung open. After chasing the animal through, he lay down by the gate.

When I came into view he attracted my attention with sharp barks and showed great delight when I closed the gate. After this, he led me to the break in the fence and then lay down. Though I looked at him and asked, "What do you want done here?" he pretended not to hear. That was none of his business!

He had much more individuality than most dogs. His reserve force and initiative usually enabled him to find a way and succeed with situations which could not be mastered in his old way. The gate opening was one of the many incidents in which these traits brought triumph.

One of his most remarkable achievements was the mastering of a number of cunning coyotes which were

Scotch at Timberline Cabin.

Scotch follows his nose.

Scotch in the yard at Long's Peak Inn.

Enos and Scotch at Long's Peak Inn, about to go on a trip.

persistent in annoying him and willing to make an opportunity to kill him. In a sunny place close to the cabin, the coyotes one autumn frequently collected for a howling concert. This irritated Scotch, and he generally chased the howlers into the woods. Now and then he lay down on the yelping grounds to prevent their prompt return. After a time these wily little wolves adopted tantalizing tactics, and one day, while Scotch was chasing the pack, a lame coyote made a detour and came behind him. In the shelter of a willow clump the coyote broke out in a maddening Babel of yelps and howls. Scotch instantly turned his back to suppress him. While he was thus busy, the entire pack doubled back into the open and taunted Scotch with attitude and howls.

Twice did the pack repeat these annoying, defying tactics. This serious situation put Scotch on his mettle. One night he went down the mountain to a ranch house fifteen miles away. For the first time he was gone all night. The next morning I was astonished to find another collie in Scotch's bed. Scotch was in a worried suspense until I welcomed the stranger; then he was most gleeful. This move on his part told plainly that he was planning something still more startling. Indeed he was, but never did I suspect what this move was to be.

That day, at the first howl of the coyotes, I rushed out to see if the visiting collie would assist Scotch. There were the coyotes in groups of two and three, yelping, howling, and watching. Both dogs were missing, but presently they came into view, cautiously approaching the coyotes from behind a screen of bushes. Suddenly the visiting collie dashed out upon them. At the same instant Scotch leaped into a willow clump and crouched down; it was by this clump that the lame coyote had each time come to howl behind Scotch.

While the visiting collie was driving the pack, the lame coyote again came out to make his sneaking flank movement. As he rounded the willow clump Scotch leaped upon him. Instantly the other dog raced back, and both dogs fell fiercely upon the coyote. Though lame, he was powerful, and finally shook the dogs off and escaped to the woods, but he was badly wounded and bleeding freely. The pack fled and came no more to howl near the cabin.

At bedtime when I went out to see the dogs, both were away. Their tracks in the road showed that Scotch had accompanied the neighboring collie at least part of the way home.

On rare occasions Scotch was allowed to go with visitors into the woods or up the mountainside. However, he was allowed to accompany only those who appreciated the companionship and the intelligence of a noble dog or who might need him to show the way home.

One day a young woman from Michigan came along and wanted to climb Long's Peak alone and without a guide. I agreed to consent to her wish if she would take Scotch with her and also first climb one of the lesser peaks on a stormy day, unaided. This climbing the young woman did, and by so doing convinced me that she had a keen sense of direction and an abundance of strength, for the day was a stormy one and the peak was completely befogged with clouds. After this there was nothing for me to do but allow her to climb Long's Peak.

Just as she was starting for Long's Peak that cool September morning, I called Scotch and said to him: "Scotch, go with this young woman up Long's Peak. Keep her on the trail, take good care of her, and stay with her until she returns!" Scotch gave a few barks of satisfaction and started with the young woman up the trail, carrying himself in a manner which indicated that he was both honored and pleased. I felt that the strength and alertness of the young woman, when combined with the faithfulness and watchfulness of Scotch, would make the ascent a success, for the dog knew the trail as well as any guide.

The young woman climbed swiftly until she reached the rocky alpine moorlands above timberline. Here she lingered long to enjoy the magnificent scenery and the brilliant flowers. It was late in the afternoon when she arrived at the summit of the Peak. After she had spent a little time there, resting and absorbing the beauty and grandeur of the scene, she started to return. She had not gone far and clouds and darkness came on, and on a slope of slide rock she turned aside from the trail.

Scotch had minded his own affairs and enjoyed himself in his own way all day long. Most of the time he had followed her closely, apparently indifferent to what happened. But the instant the young woman left the trail and started off in the wrong direction, he sprang ahead and took the lead with an alert, aggressive air. The way in which he did this should have suggested to her that he knew what he was about, but she did not appreciate this fact. She thought he had become weary and wanted to run away from her, so she called him back. Again she started in the wrong direction. This time Scotch got in front of her refused to move. She pushed him out of the way. Once more he started off in the right direction and this time she scolded him and reminded him that his master had told him to stay with her. Scotch dropped his ears, fell in behind her, and followed meekly in her steps. He had tried to carry out the first part of his master's orders; now he was resigned to the second part of them.

After going a short distance, the young woman realized that she had lost her trail but it never occurred to her that she had only to let Scotch have his way and he would lead her safely home. However, she had the good sense to stop where she was. And there, among the crags, by the stained remnants of winter's snow, thirteen thousand feet above sea level, she knew she must pass the night. The wind blew a gale and the alpine booklet turned to ice, while, in the lee of a crag, shivering with cold and hugging Scotch tight, she lay down to wait for daylight.

When darkness had come that evening and the young woman had not returned, I sent a rescue party of four guides up the Peak. They suffered much from the cold as they vainly searched among the crags through the dark hours of the windy night. Just at sunrise one of the guides found her. She was almost exhausted, but was still hugging Scotch tightly and only her fingers were frostbitten. The guide gave her wraps and food and drink, and started with her down the trail. And Scotch? Oh, as soon as the guide appeared he left her and started home for breakfast. Scotch saved this young woman's life by staying with her through the long, cold night. She appreciated the fact, and was quick to admit that if she had allowed the dog to have his own way about the trail she would have had no trouble.

Mabel Brougham and Scotch.

RISKED LIFE FOR LOVE OF NATURE

Miss Mabel Brougham, First Woman to Climb Long's Peak Without a Guide, Loses Trail and Almost Perishes in Storm.

Spends Wild Night in Lonely Fastnesses, but Was Not Dismayed, Even Though Her Toes Were Frozen.

1906

Special to The News.

ESTES PARK, Colo., Sept. 15.—All night in a storm near the summit of Long's peak was the experience Miss Mabel Brougham had as the result of winning the distinction of being the first woman to climb Long's peak alone and without a guide. During the cold night near the summit Miss Brougham suffered severely, receiving two frost bitten toes. She did not worry, however, and when seen at Long's Peak inn today was the liveliest and happiest of the guests at this well known resort for nature lovers.

"No, I did not mind it at all," said Miss Brougham after she came down the peak, accompanied by three guides, who scaled the mountain to show her the way after she had missed the trail in the storm and darkness. "I have had many happy excursions into the wilds and many strenuous experiences out with nature, she said. "So that this one, although the most severe of all, will in no way cause me to cease mingling with the outdoor world alone."

In making the climb up the peak the young lady was accompanied by Scotch, the celebrated collie dog, which is the property of the old guide, Mills, at Long's Peak inn, and it may be that to Scotch Miss Brougham owes her life, for during the long cold night the dog did his best to take care of the young lady and bring her safely home.

After gaining the summit of the peak Miss Brougham lingered so long to enjoy the world of light and shade below that darkness came upon her when she had descended but a short distance from the summit. Not comprehending the protests of Scotch, she took the wrong route and was compelled to spend a cold, windy night among the crags.

Miss Brougham is an athletic young lay of prepossessing appearance and is jolly and self-reliant. Last year she took a special course in the University of Colorado, and Monday she will leave for Chicago to spend the winter at the University of Illinois. Her home is at Sault Ste. Marie, Mich.

Mabel Brougham and Scotch
at a cabin at Long's Peak Inn.

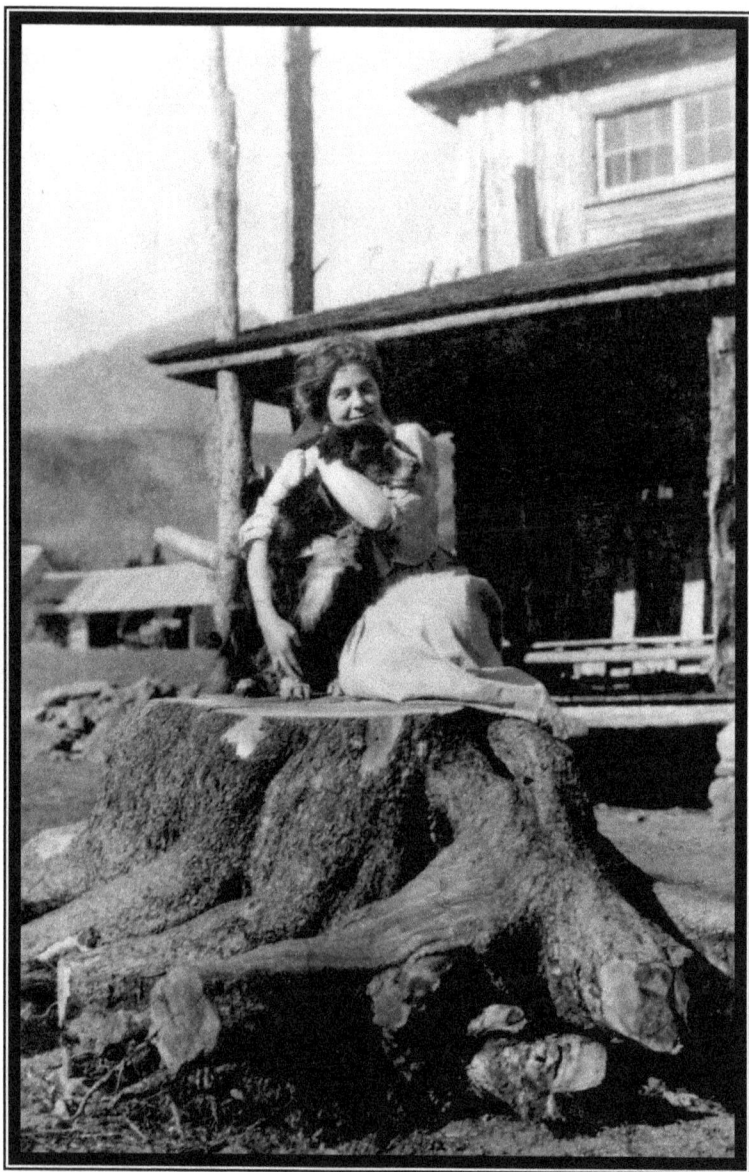

"I shall never forget," [Mabel Brougham] said,
"how delighted the dog was to find the guides.
He is a splendid fellow, like all Scotch Collies."

Mabel Brougham and Scotch.
Long's Peak is in the background.

III

One summer a family lived in a cabin at the farther side of the big yard. Scotch developed a marked fondness for the lady of the house and called on her daily. He was so purposeful about this that from the moment he rose to start there was no mistaking his plans. Along the pathway toward the cabin he went, evidently with something definite in his mind. He was going somewhere; there was no stopping, no hurrying, and no turning aside. If the door was open, in he went; if it was closed, he made a scraping stroke across it and with dignified pose waited for it to be opened. Inside he was the gentleman. Generally he made a quiet tour through all the rooms and then lay down before the fireplace. If any one talked to him, he watched the speaker and listened with pleased attention; if the speaker was animated, Scotch now and then gave a low bark of appreciation. Usually he stayed about half an hour and then went sedately out. Without looking back, he returned deliberately to his own quarters.

What an unconscious dignity there was in his make-up! He would not "jump for the gentlemen," nor leap over a stick, nor "roll over." No one ever would have thought of asking him to speak, to say grace, or to sit up on his hind legs for something to eat. All these tricks were foreign to his nature and had no place in his philosophy!

Though Scotch admitted very few to the circle of his intimate friends, he was admired, respected, and loved by thousands. One of these admirers writes of him: "Of this little rustic Inn, Scotch was no less the host than was his master. He welcomed the coming and sped the parting guest. He escorted the climbers to the beginning of the trail up Long's Peak. He received the returning trout fishermen. He kept the burros on the other side of the brook. He stood between the coyotes and the inhabitants of the chicken yard. He was always ready to play football

Enos and Scotch play football at Long's Peak Inn.

"Catching a hot liner!"

for the entertainment of the guests after dinner. He was really the busiest person about the Inn from morning till night."

Though apparently matter-of-fact and stolid, he was ever ready for a romp and was one of the most playful dogs. Except at odd times, I was the only playmate he ever had. It was a pleasure to watch him or to play with him, for he played with all his might. He took an intense delight in having me kick or toss a football for him. He raced at full speed in pursuing the ball, and upon overtaking it would try to pick it up, but it was too large for him. As soon as I picked it up, he became all alert to race after it or to leap up and intercept it. If the ball was tossed easily to him, he sprang to meet it and usually struck it with the point of his chin and sent it flying back to me; at short range we were sometimes able to sent the ball back and forth between us several times without either one moving in his tracks. If the ball was tossed above him, he leaped up to strike it with head, chin, or teeth, trying to make it bound upward; if it went up, he raced to do it over again. Occasionally he was clever enough to repeat this many times without allowing the ball to fall to the earth.

His enjoyment in make-believe play was as eager and refreshing as that of a child. This kind of play we often enjoyed in the yard. I would pretend to be searching for him, while he, crouching near in plain view, pretended to be hidden. Oh, how he enjoyed this! Again and again I would approach him from a different direction, and, when within touching distance, call, "Where is Scotch?" while he, too happy for barks, hugged the earth closely and silently. Now and then he took a pose and pretended to be looking at something far away, while all the time his eager eye was upon me. From time to time, with utmost stealth, he took a new hiding place. With ever pretense of trying not to be seen, he sometimes moved from behind me to immediately in front of me! Silently, though

"Hello, there's Scotch!"

excitedly happy, he played this delightful childish game. It always ended to his liking; I grabbed him with a "Hello, there's Scotch!" and carried him off on my shoulder.

One day a family arrived at a nearby cottage to spend the summer. During the first afternoon of their stay, the toddling baby strayed away. Every one turned out to search. With enlarging circles we covered the surrounding country and at last came upon the youngster in the woods about a quarter of a mile from the house. Scotch was with him and was lying down with head up, while the baby, asleep, was using him for a pillow, and had one chubby arm thrown across his neck. He saw us approach and lift the baby as if nothing unusual had happened.

He never failed to notice my preparations to journey beyond the mountains. Never would he watch me start on this kind of a journey, but an hour or so before leaving time he would go to the side of the house opposite where I started. Here he would refuse attention from any one and for a few days would go about sadly.

A little in advance of my homecoming, he showed that he expected me. Probably he heard my name used by the people in the house. Anyway, for two or three days before my arrival, he each evening would go down the road and wait at the place where he had greeted me many times on my return.

When I went horseback riding he was almost passionately happy if allowed to go along. Whenever my pony was brought out, he at once stopped everything and lay down near the pony to await my coming. Would I go out on the trail with him, or go to the post office and leave him behind? By the time I appeared, these questions had him in a high state of excitement. Usually he turned his head away and yawned and yawned; he rose up and sat down, altogether showing a strange combination of bashfulness and impatience; though plainly trying to be quiet, he was restless until my answer came. Usually he was able to make out what this was without waiting

Enos, Scotch, and Cricket, Enos' pony.

for any word for me. A hatchet, for example, would tell him I was going to the woods. On the other hand, the mailbag meant that I was going to the village. This meant that he could not go, whereupon he would go off slowly, lie down, and look the other way.

If the answer was "yes," he raced this way and that, leaping up once or twice to touch the pony's nose with his own. During each ride he insisted on a race with the pony; if I chanced to forget this, he never failed to remind me before the ride was over. As a reminder, he would run alongside me and leap as high as possible, then race ahead as swiftly as he could. This he repeated until I accepted his challenge. Both dog and pony gleefully enjoyed this and each tried to pass the other.

Once we were clattering over the last stretch toward home. Scotch, who was in the lead, saw our pet chicken crouched in the pony's track, where it was in danger of being crushed. Unmindful of his own danger from the pony's hoofs, he swerved, gently caught up the chicken, and lifted it out of danger. After fondling it for a moment, he raced after us at full speed.

No matter what the weather, he usually slept out-doors. He understood, however, that he was welcome to come into my cabin day or night, and was a frequent caller. In the cabin he was dignified and never used it as a piece of amusement.

IV

Scotch enjoyed being with me, and great times we had together. Many of our best days were in the wilds. Here he often suffered from hunger, cold, hardships, and sometimes from accident; yet never did he complain. Usually he endured the unpleasant things as a matter of course.

Though very lonely when left by himself, he never allowed this feeling to cause a slighting of duty. On one occasion he was supremely tried but did his duty as he understood it and was faithful under circumstances of loneliness, danger, and possible death.

At the close of one of our winter trips, Scotch and I started across the Continental Divide of the Rocky Mountains in face of weather conditions that indicated a snowstorm or a blizzard before we could gain the other side. We had eaten the last of our food twenty-four hours before, and could no longer wait for fair weather. So off we started to scale the snowy steeps of the cold, gray heights a thousand feet above. The mountains already were deeply snow-covered and it would have been a hard trip even without the discomforts and dangers of a storm.

I was on snowshoes, and for a week we had been camping and tramping through the snowy forests and glacier meadows at the source of Grand River, two miles above the sea. The primeval Rocky Mountain forests are just as near to Nature's heart in winter as in summer. I had found so much to study and enjoy that the long distance from a food supply, even when the last mouthful was eaten, had not aroused me to the seriousness of the situation. Scotch had not complained, and appeared to have the keenest collie interest in the tracks and trails, the scenes and silences away from the haunts of man. The snow lay seven feet deep, but by keeping in my snowshoe tracks Scotch easily followed me about. Our last

Scotch on a snowy trail.

camp was in the depths of an alpine forest, at an altitude of ten thousand feet. Here, though zero weather prevailed, we were easily comfortable beside a fire under the protection of an overhanging cliff.

After a walk through woods the sun came blazing in our faces past the snow-piled crags on Long's Peak, and threw slender blue shadows of the spiry spruces far out in a white glacier meadow to meet us. Re-entering the tall but open woods, we saw, down the long aisles and limb-arched avenues, a forest of tree columns, entangled in sunlight and shadow, standing on a snowy marble floor.

We were on the Pacific slope, and our plan was to cross the summit by the shortest way between timberline there and timberline on the Atlantic side. This meant ascending a thousand feet and descending an equal distance, traveling five miles amid bleak, rugged environment.

After gaining a thousand feet of altitude through the friendly forest, we climbed out and up above the trees on a steep slope at timberline. This place, the farthest up for trees, was a picturesque, desolate place. The dwarfed, gnarled, storm-shaped trees amid enormous snowdrifts told of endless, and at times deadly, struggles of the trees with the elements. Most of the trees were buried, but here and there a leaning or a storm-distorted one bent bravely above the snows.

Along the treeless, gradual ascent we started, realizing that the last steep icy climb would be dangerous and defiant. Most of the snow had slid from the steeper places, and much of the remainder had blown away. Over the unsheltered whole the wind was howling. For a time the sun shone dimly through the wind-driven snowdust that rolled from the top of the range, but it disappeared early behind wild, windswept clouds.

At last we were safe on a ridge, and we started merrily off, hoping to cover speedily the three miles of comparatively level plateau.

Scotch follows alongside Enos's snowshoe tracks.

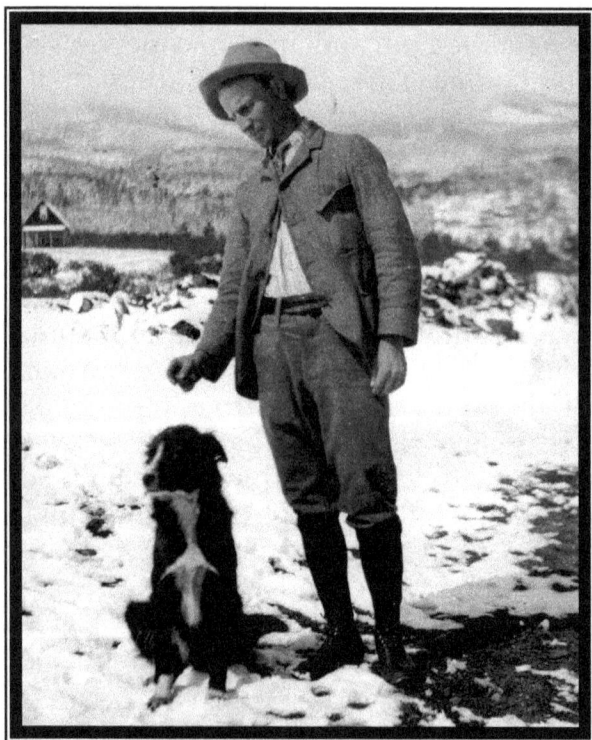

Scotch and Enos.

How the wind did blow! Up more than eleven thousand feet above the sea, with not a tree to steady or break, it had a royal sweep. The wind appeared to be putting forth its wildest efforts to blow us off the ridge. There being a broad way, I kept well from the edges. The wind came with a dash and a heavy rush, first from one quarter, then from another. I was watchful and faced each rush firmly braced. Generally this preparedness saved me; but several times the wind seemed to expand or explode beneath me, and, with an upward toss, I was flung among the icy rocks and crusted snows. Finally I took to dropping and lying flat whenever a violent gust came ripping among the crags.

There was an arctic barrenness to this alpine ridge, —not a house within miles, no trail, and here no tree could live to soften the sternness of the landscape or to cheer the traveler. The way wound amid snowy piles, icy spaces, and windswept crags.

The wind slackened and snow began to fall just as we were leaving the smooth plateau for the broken part of the divide. The next mile of way was badly cut to pieces with deep gorges from both sides of the ridge. The inner ends of several of these broke through the center of the ridge and extended beyond the ends of the gorges from the opposite side. This made the course a series of sharp, short zigzags.

We went forward in the flying snow. I could scarcely see, but felt that I could keep the way on the broken ridge between the numerous rents and canyons. On snowy, icy ledges the wind took reckless liberties. I wanted to stop but dared not, for the cold was intense enough to freeze one in a few minutes.

Fearing that a snow whirl might separate us, I fastened one end of my light, strong rope to Scotch's collar and the other end to my belt. This proved to be fortunate for both, for while we were crossing an icy, though moderate, slope, a gust of wind swept me off my feet and started us sliding. It was not steep, but was so slippery I could not stop, nor see where the slope ended, and I grabbed in vain at the few icy projections. Scotch also lost his footing and was sliding and rolling about, and the wind was hurrying us along, when I threw myself flat and dug at the ice with fingers and toes. In the midst of my unsuccessful efforts we were brought to a sudden stop by the rope between us catching over a small rock point that was thrust up through the ice. Around this in every direction was smooth, sloping ice; this, with the high wind, made me wonder for a moment how we were to get safely off the slope. The belt axe proved the means, for with it I reached out as far as I could and chopped a hole in the ice, while with the other hand I clung to the rock-point. Then, returning the axe to my belt, I caught hold in the chopped place and pulled myself forward, repeating this until on safe footing.

In oncoming darkness and whirling snow I had safely rounded the ends of two gorges and was hurrying forward over a comparatively level stretch, with the wind at my back boosting me along. Scotch was running by my side and evidently was trusting me to guard against all dangers. This I tried to do. Suddenly, however, there came a fierce dash of wind and whirl of snow that hid everything. Instantly I flung myself flat, trying to stop quickly. Just as I did this I caught the strange, weird sound made by high wind as it sweeps across a canyon, and at once realized that we were close to a storm-hidden gorge. I stopped against a rock, while Scotch slid into the chasm and was hauled back with the rope.

The gorge had been encountered between two out-thrusting side gorges, and between these in the darkness I had a cold time feeling my way out. At last I came to a cairn of stones that I recognized. I had missed the way by only a few yards, but this miss had been nearly fatal.

Not daring to hurry in the darkness in order to get warm, I was becoming colder every moment. I still had a stiff climb between me and the summit, with timberline three rough miles beyond. To attempt to make it would probably result in freezing or tumbling into a gorge. At last I realized that I must stop and spend the night in a snowdrift. Quickly kicking and trampling a trench in a loose drift, I placed my elkskin sleeping bag therein, thrust Scotch into the bag, and then squeezed into it myself.

I was almost congealed with cold. My first thought after warming up was to wonder why I had not earlier remembered the bag. Two in a bag would guarantee warmth, and with warmth, a snowdrift on the crest of the continent would not be a bad place in which to lodge for the night.

The sounds of wind and snow beating upon the bag grew fainter and fainter as we were drifted and piled over with the snow. At the same time our temperature rose, and before long it was necessary to open the flap of the bag slightly for ventilation.

At last the sounds of the storm could barely be heard. Was the storm quieting down, or was its roar muffled and lost in the deepening cover of snow? was the unimportant question occupying my thoughts when I fell asleep.

Scotch awakened me in trying to get out of the bag. It was morning. Out we crawled, and, standing with only my head above the drift, I found the air still and saw a snowy mountain world all serene in the morning sun. I hastily adjusted sleeping bag and snowshoes, and we set off for the final climb to the summit.

The final hundred feet or so rose steep, jagged, and ice covered before me. There was nothing to lay hold of; every point of vantage was plated with smooth ice. There appeared only one way to surmount this icy barrier and that was to chop toe- and hand-holds from the bottom to the top of this icy wall, which in places was close to vertical. Such a climb would not be especially difficult or dangerous for me, but could Scotch do it? He could hardly know how to place his feet in the holes or on the steps properly; nor could he realize that a slip or a misstep would mean a slide and a roll to death.

Leaving the sleeping bag and snowshoes with Scotch, I grasped my axe and shopped my way to the top and then went down and carried bag and snowshoes up. Returning for Scotch, I started him climbing just ahead of me, so that I could boost and encourage him. We had gained only a few feet when it became plain that sooner or later he would slip and bring disaster to both of us. We stopped and descended to the bottom for a new start.

Though the wind was again blowing a gale, I determined to carry him. His weight was forty pounds, and he would make a top-heavy load and give the wind a good chance to upset my balance and tip me off the wall. But, as there appeared no other way, I threw him over my shoulder and started up.

Many times Scotch and I had been in ticklish places together, and more than once I had pulled him up rocky cliffs on which he could not find footing. Several times I had carried him over gulches on fallen logs that were too slippery for him. He was so trusting and so trained that he relaxed and never moved while in my arms or on my shoulder.

Arriving at the place least steep, I stopped to transfer Scotch from one shoulder to the other. The wind was at its worst; its direction frequently changed and it alternately calmed and then came on like an explosion. For several seconds it had been roaring down the slope; bracing myself to withstand its force from this direction, I was about to move Scotch, when it suddenly shifted to one side and came with the force of a breaker. It threw me off my balance and tumbled me heavily against the icy slope.

Though my head struck solidly, Scotch came down beneath me and took most of the shock. Instantly we glanced off and began to slide swiftly. Fortunately I managed to get two fingers into one of the chopped holes and held fast. I clung to Scotch with one arm; we came to a stop, both saved. Scotch gave a yelp of pain when he fell beneath me, but he did not move. Had he made a jump or attempted to help himself, it is likely that both of us would have gone to the bottom of the slope.

Gripping Scotch with one hand and clinging to the icy hold with the other, I shuffled about until I got my feet into two holes in the icy wall. Standing in these and leaning against the ice, with the wind butting and dashing, I attempted the ticklish task of lifting Scotch again to my shoulder—and succeeded. A minute later we paused to breathe on the summit's icy ridge, between two oceans and amid seas of snowy peaks.

Enos, Scotch, and Cricket.

ᴅ

One cold winter day we were returning from a four day's trip on the Continental Divide, when, a little above timberline, I stopped to take some photographs. To do this it was necessary for me to take off my sheepskin mittens, which I placed in my coat pocket, but not securely, as it proved. From time to time, as I climbed to the summit of the Divide, I stopped to take photographs, but on the summit the cold pierced my silk gloves and I felt for my mittens, to find one of them was lost. I stooped, put an arm around Scotch and told him that I had lost a mitten and that I wanted him to go down for it to save me the trouble. "It won't take you very long," I said, "but it will be a hard trip for me. Go and fetch it to me."

Instead of starting off quickly and willingly as he had invariably done before in obedience to my commands, he stood still. His eager, alert ears drooped. He did not make a move. I repeated the command in my most kindly tones. At this, instead of starting down the mountain for the mitten, he slunk slowly away toward home. Apparently he did not want to climb down the steep, icy slope of a mile to timberline, more than a thousand feet below. I thought he misunderstood me, so I called him back, patted him, and then, pointing down the slope, said, "Go for the mitten, Scotch; I will wait for you here." He started, but went unwillingly. He had always served me so cheerfully that I could not understand his behavior, and it was not until later that I realized how cruelly he had misunderstood.

The summit of the Continental divide where I stood when I sent Scotch back, was a very rough and lonely region. On every hand were broken, snowy peaks and rugged canyons. My cabin, eighteen miles away, was the nearest house, and the region was utterly wild.

I waited a reasonable time for Scotch to return, but he did not come back. Thinking he might have gone by without my seeing him, I walked some distance along the summit, first in one direction and then in the other, but, seeing neither him nor his tracks, I knew that he had not yet returned. As it was late in the afternoon and growing colder, I decided to go slowly on toward my cabin. I started along a route I felt sure he would follow and I reasoned that he would overtake me. Darkness came on and still no Scotch, but I kept on going forward. For the remainder of the way I told myself that he might have got by me in the darkness.

When, at midnight, I arrived at the cabin, I expected to be greeted by him. He was not there. I felt that something was wrong and feared that he had met with an accident. I slept two hours and rose, but he was still missing. I decided to tie on my snowshoes and go to meet him. The thermometer showed fourteen degrees below zero.

I started at three o'clock in the morning, feeling that I should meet him before going far. I kept on and on and when at noon I arrived at the place on the summit from which I had sent him back, Scotch was not there to cheer the wintry, silent scene.

Slowly I made my way down the slope and at two in the afternoon, twenty-four hours after I had sent Scotch down the mountain, I paused on a crag and looked below. There, in a world of white, Scotch lay by the mitten in the snow. He had misunderstood me and had gone back to guard the mitten instead of to get it.

He could hardly contain himself for joy when we met. He leaped into the air, barked, rolled over, licked my hand, whined, seized the mitten in his mouth, raced round and round me, and did everything that an alert, affectionate, faithful dog could to show that he appreciated my appreciation of his supremely faithful services.

After waiting for him to eat a luncheon we started for home, where we arrived at one o'clock in the morning. Had I not gone back for Scotch, I suppose he would have died beside the mitten. Without food or companionship, in a region cold, cheerless, and oppressive, he was watching the mitten because he had understood that I had told him to watch it. In the annals of the dog I do not know of any more touching instance of loyalty.

Waiting to go for a ride

VI

Through the seasons and through the years Scotch and I wandered in the wilds and enjoyed nature together. Though we were often wet, hungry, or cold, he never ceased to be cheerful. Through the scenes and the silences we went side by side; side by side in the lonely night we gazed into the campfire, and in feeling lived strangely through "yesterday's seven thousand years" together.

He was only a puppy the first time that he went with me to enjoy the woods. During this trip we came upon an unextinguished campfire that was spreading and about to become a forest fire. Upon this fire I fell with utmost speed so as to extinguish it before it should enlarge beyond control. My wild stampings, beatings, and hurling of firebrands made a deep impression on puppy Scotch. For a time he stood still and watched me, and then he jumped in and tried to help. He bit and clawed at the flames, burned himself, and with deep growlings, desperately shook smoking sticks.

The day following this incident, as we strolled through the woods, he came upon another smouldering campfire and at once called my attention to it with lively barking. I patted him and tried to make him understand that I appreciated what he had done, and then extinguished the fire. Through the years, in our wood wanderings, he was alert for fire and prompt to warn me of a discovery. His nose and eye detected many fires that even my trained and watchful senses had missed.

One autumn, while watching a forest fire, we became enveloped in smoke and narrowly escaped with our lives. The fire had started in the bottom and was burning upward in the end of a long, wide mountain valley, and giving off volumes of smoke. In trying to obtain a clearer view, and also to avoid the smoke, we descended into a ravine close behind the fire. Shortly after our arrival a strong wind drove the wings of the fire outward to right and left, then backward down both sides of the valley, filling the ravine with smoke.

This movement of the fire would in a short time have encircled us with flames. I made a dash to avoid this peril, and in running along a rock ledge in the smoke, stumbled into a rocky place and one of my shoes stuck fast. This threw me heavily and badly sprained my left leg. Amid thick smoke, falling ashes, and approaching flames, this situation was a serious one. Scotch showed the deepest concern by staying close by me and finally by giving a number of strange barks such as I had never before heard. After freeing myself I was unable to walk, and in hopping and creeping along, my camera became so annoying that I gave it to Scotch; but in the brush the straps became so often entangled that throwing it away proved a relief to us both.

Meanwhile we were making slow progress through the unburned woods and the fire was roaring close. Seeing no hope of getting out of the way, we finally took refuge to the leeward side of a rocky crag where the flames could not reach us. But could we avoid being smothered? Already we were dangerously near that and the fire had yet to surge around us. To send Scotch for water offered a possible means of escape. Slapping my coat upon the rocks two or three times I commanded, "Water, Scotch, water!" He understood, and with an eager bark seized the coat and vanished in the smoke. He would be compelled to pass through a line of flame in order to reach the water in the ravine, but this he would do or die.

After waiting a reasonable time I began to call, "Scotch! Scotch!" as loudly as my parched throat and gasping permitted. Presently he leaped upon me, fearfully burned but with the saturated coat in his teeth.

Most of his shaggy coat was seared off, one eye was

closed, and there was a cruel burn on his left side. Hurriedly I bound a coat sleeve around his head to protect his eyes and nose, then squeezed enough water from the coat to wet my throat. Hugging Scotch closely, I spread the wet coat over us both and covered my face with a wet handkerchief. With stifling smoke and fiery heat the flames surged around, but at last swept over and left us both alive. Without the help from Scotch I must have perished.

It was this useful fire fighting habit that caused the death of my faithful Scotch. One morning the men started off to do some road work. Scotch saw them go and apparently wanted to go with them. I had just returned from a long absence and had to stay in the cabin and write letters. About half an hour after the men had gone, Scotch gave a scratching knock at the door. Plainly he wanted to follow the men and had come for my consent to go without me. I patted him and urged him to go. He left the cabin, never again to return.

Scotch arrived at the road work just as the men had lighted and run away from a blast. He saw the smoking fuse and sprang to extinguish it, as the blast exploded. He was killed instantly.

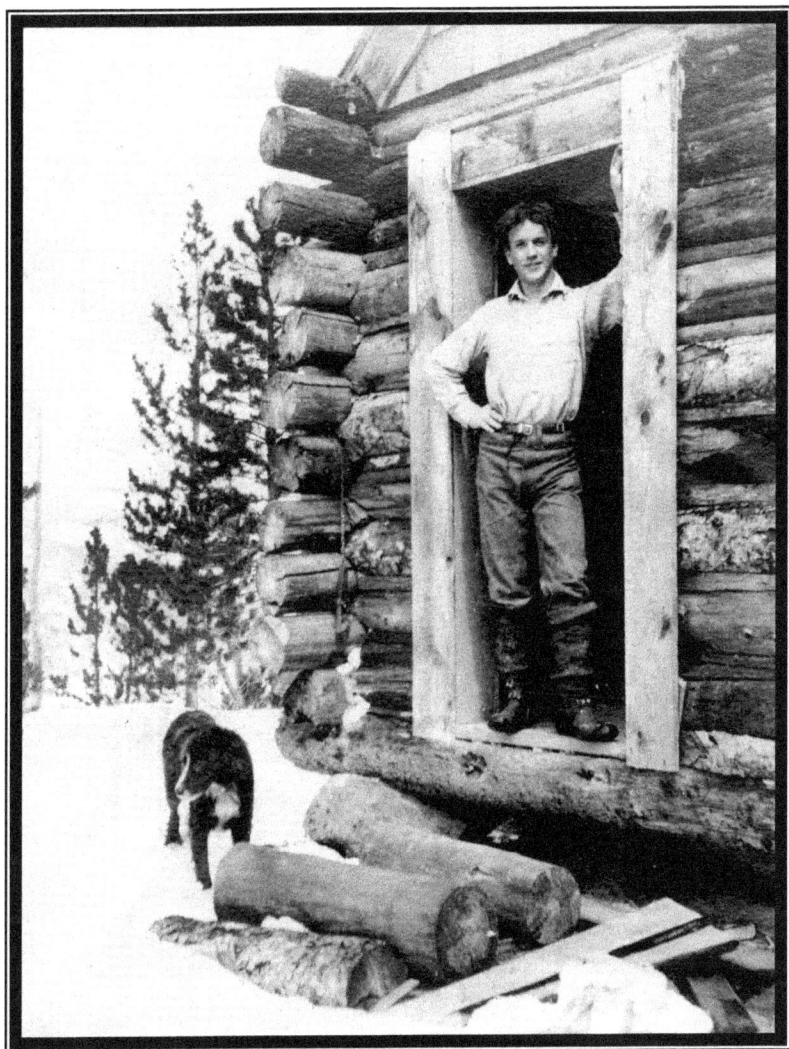

Scotch and Joe (Enoch) Mills, Enos' younger brother,
at Joe's homestead.

DAUNTLESS UNIVERSITY GIRL
PERFORMS AN AMAZING FEAT

TO ENJOY UNDISTURBED THE GLORIOUS VIEW SHE CLIMBED LONG'S PEAK WITHOUT A GUIDE.

MISS MAUDE V. BROUGHAM,
Michigan girl who spent a night on Long's Peak with a dog as her sole companion.

BOULDER, Colo., Sept. 18.—(Special.) —Miss Maud V. Brougham of Sault Ste. Marie, Mich., who was a freshman at the University of Colorado last year, spent the summer in Colorado, and leaves the state with a thrilling experience as a climax of her many daring undertakings.

Last week while at Mills' Inn at Estes Park she planned to climb Long's Peak without a guide. She took with her a Scotch collie belonging to Mr. Mills. She found the "keyhole," followed the trail to the "trough" and climbed to the top without incident. There was a great deal of snow and ice on the trail and the last 200 feet of smooth rock on a sharp slope were perilous indeed. The view over the range enraptured her and she lingered on the summit to watch the sunset. A little before 4 o'clock she realized she must return. Reaching the narrows, 200 feet from the summit, she lost the trail and wandered about until she struck the trough again. It was now quite dark and all thought of descending farther was abandoned. With the faithful dog she sought an overhanging rock and settled down to spend the night. She had no blanket, or means of making a fire,

and knew that it would be folly to attempt to retrace her steps. She fixed herself as comfortably as possible, but had it not been for the dog she probably would have frozen. As it was her toes were frozen, and her right arm, from the elbow to the wrist, which she had leaned upon a rock, was badly frosted.

Friends at the inn became alarmed and guides were sent to search for her. They believed that she had fallen from a cliff. When darkness overtook them they built a campfire, planning to resume the search in the morning. Throughout the night they called aloud, hoping for a answer.

At daylight Miss Brougham started on the down trail and came upon the searchers, who were astonished to find her alive and uninjured.

"I shall never forget," she said, "how delighted the dog was to find the guides. He is a splendid fellow, like all Scotch Collies."

The guides and Miss Brougham camped but a little way apart, but Miss Brougham, being around a bend and behind a rock, did not hear their cries.

Miss Brougham was enthusiastic in describing the climb and her thrilling adventure.

ENOS MILLS' COLLIE COLORADO HERO

✤✤ ✤✤ ✤✤ ✤✤ ✤✤   ✤✤ ✤✤ ✤✤ ✤✤ ✤✤

Gallant Little Dog Knew Danger of Forest Fires and Died Fighting Sparks

BY ALBERT PAYSON TERHUNE

PERHAPS you have read tihs story in book form. It was printed, years ago, and it deserved more fame than it won. It was by Enos Mills, Colorado naturalist, and peerless outdoor man. In it he told the true life-tale of his little black collie, Scotch. Here in that tale:

A farmer gave the puppy to Mills, and the new owner carried the gift home in his overcoat pocket. "Home," just then, was a cabin high in the Rocky Mountains, near Estes Park, Colo. There was an old tub on the cabin porch. Scotch chose this as his bedroom, nor did he leave it for the pleasanter kennel that was made for him.

The tub gave him all the room he wanted and enabled him to see in every direction. From it he barked loud defiance at any strangers who might be coming along the trail.

He feared only one thing in the world, and that fear was well founded. A neighbor stopped at the cabin. Scotch trotted out to make friends with the long-eared little burro the visitor had ridden. The burro kicked him half to death. Thenceforth the puppy would scamper under the porch at first sight of an approaching burro.

Scotch's chief playmate was a young grizzly bear named Johnny, which Mills had tamed. By the hour these ill-assorted chums would romp together, roughly, but in perfect good humor. The bear seemed to take a delight in biting Scotch's fluffy tail. Scotch would retaliate by nipping Johnny's sensitive nose. Then a lively romp would begin.

The little black collie's education began early. Mills talked to him as if to a child, teaching him the meanings of simple words, so that presently Scotch could bring his master any household article or camp utensil the latter bade him fetch. He had a natural genius, too, as a cattle driver, and was as valuable along this line as any hired man. He taught himself

-44-

to open pasture gates and drive cattle thru.

Coyotes menaced the ranch's chicken yards. Between these skulking brutes and Scotch there was a lifelong feud. But he more than matched their craftiness with his own keen common sense, and he balked their cleverest efforts to get at the Mills poultry. Small as he was, he was tough and wiry and a natural-born fighter. No coyote was his equal in battle.

Once a baby, barely able to walk, toddled away into the forest from a neighbor's cabin. Nor could any of the hastily-summoned human searchers find the lost child. All the parents knew was that their baby was lost somewhere in the woods and was at the mercy of any coyote or wolf.

Then Scotch's services were called upon. Without the slightest hesitation, he dashed into the forest and led the search party to the sleeping child.

By sheer reasoning power he learned to know in which direction Mills might be going whenever the latter set forth from the cabin. If Mills were carrying an ax, Scotch darted ahead to the woods, knowing there was going to be a day of wood-chopping. If Mills were carrying the mailbag, Scotch would gallop ahead of him in the direction of the post-office.

Forest fires are ever a peril in that wild region. Scotch saw Mills fight one of these blazes while the collie was only a pup. That was enough for the wise little dog. From that time on whenever he caught the whiff of distant smoke in the woods he would go to investigate it and then rush back to Mills and lead him to the spot where the conflagration was starting. In this way many a forest fire was put out before it could grow large enough to do real damage to the timber.

In an effort to save his master from death, when Mills had broken an ankle during a fire-fight and could not crawl fast enough out of danger, the dog was almost burned to death. Scotch could readily have saved himself by flight, but he would not leave Mills nor let up on his efforts to rescue the man who was his god.

At sight of even a few sparks in an abandoned campfire in the woods Scotch always flew at the embers and patted them out with his paws or else bit savagely at them. It was almost a mania with him, this self-imposed duty to extinguish fires wherever he might find them.

One day a party of men were on a blasting job, not far from the cabin, in an attempt to clear the rocks away for the building of a mountain road. Scotch watched them with interest as they filed past the cabin. He was inquisitive as to what they might be planning to do. He trotted anxiously back to the room where his master was at work.

I am going to tell the rest of the happening in Mills' own words, as found on the final page of his beautiful book, "The Story of Scotch." Mills wrote:

"Scotch gave a scratching knock at the door. Plainly he wanted to follow the men, and had come to me for my consent to go without me. I patted his head and urged him to go.

"He left the cabin, never again to return.

"Scotch arrived at the road-work just as the men had lighted and run away from a blast. He saw the smoking fuse and sprang to extinguish it as the blast exploded. He was instantly killed."

He led the search.

Illustration from the Rocky Mountain News article from
Sunday, August 17, 1930.

Dear Mr. Mills,

Your kind letter was forwarded to me at my other home in
Montgomery, Alabama, where I am spending the winter. I thank you very
much for your photograph and the book. The picture has not come; but I am
proud to possess it as a gift from you. It makes me feel as if we had
met and added to our occasional exchange of messages the warmth of a
cordial handshake. I look forward eagerly to reading "The Story of
Scotch." It will be like a breath of life-giving mountain air.

I hope you will have a happy Christmas "in the heart of the Rockies
with the pines, birds and wild-flowers." I know that "Nature never did
betray the heart that trusted her," and I am sure she will fill the New
Year for you with beauty and gladness.

With cordial greetings, I am,

Sincerely yours,

Helen Keller

Montgomery, Alabama,

December eighth.

ARTHUR S. BENT
ESTABLISHED 1886
GENERAL CONTRACTOR

Los Angeles   Oct. 10th 1910
                          Monday

Enos A. Mills   Esq.
Estes Park,   Colo.,

Dear Mr. Mills:-

My boy and girl want to know what was the final fate of
"**Scotch**" if he be not still with you.

Some years ago a man drove from Los Angeles to Yosemite
Valley with his family which included a Collie. Half
way there a pair of discarded shoes which had been worn
by the little boy, were thrown from the Camp Wagon one
evening. The next morning the dog was missing and
after calling in vain they concluded he must have left
for home in the night, and went on their way sorrowing
for fear they would never see him again.

Three weeks later returning over the same road they were
met by their joyous dog near a farm house and on inquiring
found he had taken his station by the little shoes and
had steadily refused to be coaxed aaway, until finding he
was likely to starve there in the road the farmer managed
to get the shoes to the house where he followed and had
lived.

"Bob"Kermack up at Magnolia, Colorado has some fine
collies. One of them can be sent out from the house
by Mrs. Kermack with a note and will find him anywhere on
the trails of Boulder Cañon.- sometimes a long quest.

When **we** read your very interesting book we always begin
with the last chapter as being the best introduction to
the whole.

                     Sincerely yours,

ASB/L

Grand Lake, Colorado, Jan. 30, 1917.

My dear Mr. Mills:

I am sending with this what additional notes I could
get, to-gether with a few pictures.   I can get all sorts of scenic pictures, but thought you might prefer the historical ones. I have written
on the back of each what it represents.   You asked about the depth
of the lake, but I have been unable to get an accurate report. The
reported soundings vary from 250 to 700 feet as the greatest depth.
I have been unable to get anything, either, regarding Rocky Mountain
Jim, at least, nothing definite enough to write about.

We have just finished reading your Story of Scotch, and I
cannot tell you how much we have enjoyed.it. My little daughter w.s especially interested, as she loves a dog above anything. From reading
your delightful books it seems that I know you better than I do many
people that I see every day.   Mr. Cairns and I would both be so glad
if you would come over any time that you feel that you can.   Since
our home burned, we are living in one of our little cottages, but it is
not so tiny but what there is always room for our friends.

With very best wishes, I am

Sincerely yours,

Mary L. Cairns.

My dear Mr.Mills;

How I wish I sould reach across space and take your hand! I'd be so proud. I do not know how to begin to thank you for the pleasure you have given me and the "Deacon." First I read your book myself,to get the hang of it,and now I am reading it aloud to my family. Without one dissenting voice,(there are three of us,him and me and my secretary,) we agree that the Old Pine chapter is the very most intersting thing we ever read in all our lives. There are many,many other places where I stop and go back and read it over again to be sure that I have lost nothing in atmosphere,color and word value. I find your English unusually strong and pure,and enjoy that feature of your book. Before I had read a dozen pages my husband interrupted me to say,"He phrases well!"

There is only one dog in all the world I like better than yours. I can't take "Stickeen," from his pedestal,because he was so little and so individual. But "Scotch" has second place,crowded close up. I have a way of thinking of you and John Muir together;and the dogs might as well be grouped as the masters. When I read your books,what I do appears almost silly , to me. There have been times when the quicksands caught my feet and began their fatal sucking,when I mired past ability to extricate myself,when the sun blistered through my clothing,that I thought I was having a pretty strenuous time. But when I read the records that such men as you and Muir write,my dealings with nature appeal to me about like a child playing in the back yard.

Never-the-less,because you have been good enough to say you cared for my work,I am going to send you one book more. It is very much the best I have done and is fiction in name only. I hope you will like it one tenth as much as I like the book you so kindly sent me.

Sincerely yours,

Limberlost Cabin,
Geneva,Indiana.
March 6, 1910.

Gene Stratton Porter.